THE ART OF STRATEGIC SOCIAL MEDIA MARKETING

Mastering Strategies for Effective Digital Advertising

Kimberly Hodge

DISCLAIMER

The information provided in this book is for general informational purposes only and does not constitute financial advice. The author and publisher are not responsible for any actions or decisions made based on the content of this book. Readers are advised to seek professional financial advice before making any investment or financial decisions.

The content of this book is based on the author's research and personal experiences, and it may not be suitable for every individual's financial situation. The author and publisher make no representations or warranties of any kind, express or implied, about the completeness, accuracy, reliability, suitability, or availability of the information contained in this book.

Any reliance you place on such information is, therefore, strictly at your own risk. In no event will the author or publisher be liable for any loss or damage including, without limitation, indirect or consequential loss or damage, or any loss or damage whatsoever arising from loss of data or profits arising out of or in connection with the use of this book.

CONTENTS

INTRODUCTION:

In today's digital landscape, social media advertising has become increasingly important in reaching and engaging with a wide audience. With the ever-growing number of people using social media platforms, businesses can no longer afford to overlook the power of social media advertising.

Firstly, social media advertising allows businesses to target specific demographics and interests with precision. Platforms like Facebook, Instagram, and LinkedIn offer advanced targeting options that enable businesses to reach their ideal audience based on factors such as age, location, interests, and even online behaviors. This level of targeting ensures that businesses can deliver their messages to those who are most likely to be interested in their products or services, increasing the chances of conversion and return on investment.

Secondly, social media advertising provides a cost-effective way for businesses to promote their brand and offerings. Compared to traditional advertising methods, such as TV or print ads, social media advertising can be much more budget friendly. Businesses can set their advertising budgets and determine how much they are willing to spend on campaigns. Additionally, the ability to track and analyze the performance of social media ads in real-time allows businesses to adjust and optimize their campaigns for maximum impact.

Furthermore, social media advertising allows for increased brand visibility and awareness. With a strong social media presence, businesses can showcase their products and services to a vast audience, potentially reaching millions of users. Through engaging content, captivating visuals, and interactive ads, businesses can effectively capture the attention of users and leave a lasting impression. This increased visibility not only helps businesses attract new customers but also fosters brand loyalty and encourages repeat business.

Lastly, social media advertising enables businesses to engage and interact with their audience on a more personal level. Through comments, likes, and shares, businesses can create a sense of community and foster meaningful connections with their customers. This interaction not only humanizes the brand but also allows businesses to gather valuable feedback, insights, and customer preferences, which can be used to improve products, services, and overall customer experience.

In conclusion, social media advertising plays a crucial role in today's digital landscape. It offers businesses the opportunity to reach a targeted audience, cost-effectively promote their brand, increase visibility and engagement, and ultimately drive business growth. By harnessing the power of social media advertising, businesses can stay relevant, competitive, and connected in an increasingly digital world.

CHAPTER 1: UNDERSTANDING SOCIAL MEDIA MARKETING

In today's digital age, the world of social media advertising has revolutionized the way businesses engage with their target audience. With billions of active users, platforms such as Facebook, Instagram, and Twitter offer a vast playground for brands to showcase their products or services. But why is it so important for businesses to harness the power of social media advertising?

First and foremost, social media advertising allows businesses to reach a highly targeted and specific audience. Unlike traditional advertising methods, where companies cast a wide net and hope for the best, social media platforms offer advanced targeting options. Businesses can narrow down their audience based on demographics, interests, behaviors, and even past purchase history. This level of precision ensures that your ads are shown to those who are most likely to be interested in what you have to offer.

Additionally, social media advertising provides an unparalleled opportunity for businesses to engage and interact with their audience. By creating compelling content, brands can foster a sense of community and build trust with their customers. With features like comments, direct messages, and shareability, businesses can directly communicate with their audience and address their needs or concerns. This two-way communication not only strengthens the brand-consumer relationship but also provides valuable insights and feedback for businesses to improve their offerings.

Furthermore, social media advertising offers a cost-effective alternative to traditional advertising channels. With a range of budgeting options, businesses can set a comfortable ad spend that aligns with their financial goals. Compared to traditional media outlets like TV or radio, social media advertising provides measurable results and a higher return on investment. Detailed analytics and reporting tools allow businesses to track key metrics such as reach, engagement, and conversion rates, enabling them to optimize their campaigns for maximum impact.

In today's competitive market, staying ahead of the curve is essential for business success. Social media advertising not only enables businesses to increase their brand visibility but also gives them a competitive edge. With the ability to analyze data and target specific demographics, businesses can fine-tune their strategies and ensure their messages are reaching the right people at the right time. By leveraging the exciting world of social media advertising, businesses can connect with their audience on a deeper level, expand their reach, and ultimately drive growth and success.

Importance of Social Media Advertising

Social media advertising plays a crucial role in today's digital landscape.

Here's why:

Extensive Reach: Social media platforms like Facebook, Instagram, Twitter, and LinkedIn have billions of active users. Advertising on these platforms allows businesses to reach a wide and diverse audience, irrespective of geographical boundaries.

Targeted Advertising: Social media platforms provide sophisticated targeting options based on demographics, interests, behaviors, and connections. This enables businesses to tailor their advertisements to specific target audiences, increasing the chances of reaching potential customers.

Cost-Effective: Compared to traditional advertising methods, social media advertising offers cost-effective options for businesses of all sizes. With customizable budgets and bidding models, businesses have control over their ad spending and can achieve desired results without breaking the bank.

Data Insights: Social media platforms provide detailed analytics and performance metrics that help businesses measure the effectiveness of their advertising campaigns. This data allows for continuous improvement and optimization, ensuring that marketing efforts are focused on strategies that yield the best results.

Increased Brand Awareness: Social media advertising allows businesses to effectively build and increase brand awareness. By regularly appearing on users' newsfeeds and timelines, businesses can stay top-of-mind and enhance brand recognition.

Engagement and Interactivity: Social media platforms encourage user engagement through likes, comments, shares, and direct messages. This provides an opportunity for businesses to interact with their audience, build relationships, address queries, and gather valuable feedback.

Mobile Accessibility: With the widespread use of smartphones, social media platforms have become easily accessible to users on the go. This means that businesses can reach and engage with their target audience anytime, anywhere, increasing the chances of converting leads into customers.

In conclusion, social media advertising is essential in today's digital landscape due to its wide reach, targeted capabilities, cost-effectiveness, data insights, brand building potential, engagement opportunities, and mobile accessibility. By leveraging these platforms effectively, businesses can significantly boost their online presence and drive tangible results.

Social media platforms have undeniably transformed into key marketing channels for businesses in recent years. With the extensive reach and active user base on platforms like Facebook, Instagram, Twitter, and LinkedIn, companies now have unprecedented opportunities to connect with their target audience, build brand awareness, and drive sales.

Firstly, social media provides a vast user base, with millions of individuals actively engaging with content every day. This provides businesses with a tremendous opportunity to reach a large number of potential customers. By strategically creating and sharing engaging content, businesses can capture the attention of their target audience and increase brand visibility.

Additionally, social media platforms offer powerful targeting capabilities, allowing businesses to narrow down their reach to specific demographics, interests, and behaviors. This enables companies to deliver personalized messages tailored to individual consumers, resulting in higher conversion rates and more effective marketing campaigns.

Furthermore, social media platforms have advanced analytics and insights tools that offer valuable data on user behavior, demographics, and engagement metrics. This data enables businesses to track the performance of their marketing efforts, identify trends, and make data-driven decisions to optimize their strategies.

Moreover, social media platforms provide opportunities for direct customer engagement. Brands can use features such as comments, direct messages, and live chat to interact with customers in real-time, address their concerns, and build meaningful relationships. This personalized approach enhances customer satisfaction and fosters loyalty.

Lastly, social media platforms offer various advertising options, including sponsored posts, influencer partnerships, and targeted ads, allowing businesses to amplify their reach and increase the effectiveness of their marketing campaigns. These advertising options provide businesses with the ability to target specific audiences and maximize their return on investment.

In conclusion, with their extensive user base, advanced targeting capabilities, analytics tools, and opportunities for direct customer engagement, social media platforms have become indispensable marketing channels for businesses. By strategically leveraging these platforms, companies can boost their brand visibility, engage with their target audience, and ultimately drive

Empowering Businesses to Create Successful Advertising Campaigns

As a business, it's essential to harness the power of platforms like Facebook, Instagram, Twitter, and LinkedIn to create successful advertising campaigns.

Here's how you can empower your business to do just that:

Set clear goals: Before diving into social media advertising, define your goals. Do you want to increase brand awareness, generate leads, or drive sales? This will guide your campaign strategy.

Know your target audience: Understanding your target audience is key to designing effective ads. Analyze demographics, interests, and online behavior to create tailored messages that resonate.

Create engaging content: Social media platforms thrive on eye-catching visuals and compelling copy. Invest time in creating high-quality, attention-grabbing content that tells your brand story and connects with your audience.

Optimize for mobile: Mobile devices dominate social media usage, so ensure your ads are mobile-friendly. Use concise, easy-to-read text and optimize visuals for smaller screens to maximize engagement.

Utilize targeting options: Social media platforms offer advanced targeting options to reach the right audience. Utilize parameters such as location, interests, demographics, and behavior to target your ads effectively.

Test and optimize: Don't settle for one ad. Experiment with different variations, such as headlines, visuals, and calls to action. Regularly monitor and analyze campaign performance to identify what's working and what needs improvement.

Set a budget and monitor spending: Establish a budget that aligns with your goals and constantly monitor your spending. Learn from the data and allocate more funds to the ads that deliver the best results.

Leverage tracking and analytics: Use tracking pixels, conversion tracking, and social media analytics tools to measure the success of your campaigns. This data will provide valuable insights to optimize future efforts.

Engage with your audience: Social media advertising offers an opportunity to directly engage with your audience. Respond to comments, messages, and reviews promptly to build trust and foster brand loyalty.

Stay updated on trends: Social media platforms constantly evolve, introducing new features and algorithms. Stay updated with the latest trends, best practices, and changes to ensure your campaigns stay effective and relevant.

By following these strategies, you can empower your business to create successful social media advertising campaigns that captivate your audience, drive meaningful results, and ultimately boost your bottom line. Good luck!

Benefits of Effective Social Media Advertising

Effective social media advertising offers numerous benefits for businesses.

Here are a few key advantages:

Increased brand visibility: Social media platforms have billions of active users, providing businesses with a vast audience to showcase their brand and reach potential customers.

Targeted advertising: Social media platforms allow businesses to target specific demographics and interests, ensuring that ads are seen by the right audience. This helps to maximize the effectiveness of advertising campaigns and increase conversion rates.

Cost-effective: Compared to traditional advertising channels, social media advertising is often more affordable. Businesses can set their own budget and choose between cost-per-click (CPC) or cost-per-impression (CPM) models, allowing for better control over spending.

Enhanced engagement: Social media advertising opens opportunities for direct interaction with customers through comments, likes, shares, and messages. This allows businesses to build relationships, address concerns, and receive valuable feedback.

Increased website traffic and conversions: By linking ads to specific landing pages, businesses can drive targeted traffic to their website and increase the likelihood of conversions, such as purchases or sign-ups.

Measurable results: Social media advertising platforms provide comprehensive analytics and reporting tools that allow businesses to track the performance of their ads. This data can be used to refine strategies and optimize future campaigns.

Overall, effective social media advertising can significantly expand a business's reach, engage with the target audience, and drive tangible results in terms of brand awareness, customer engagement, and conversions.

Social media platforms have become powerful advertising tools, allowing businesses to reach a wide audience and promote their products or services.

Here's an overview of some popular social media platforms and their advertising capabilities:

Facebook: With over 2.8 billion monthly active users, Facebook offers robust advertising options. Businesses can create targeted ads based on demographics, interests, and behaviors. Facebook's ad manager provides various ad formats, including image ads, video ads, carousel ads, and more. Additionally, Facebook offers features like custom audience targeting, lookalike audience targeting, and retargeting.

Instagram: As a subsidiary of Facebook, Instagram also offers extensive advertising opportunities. Businesses can create visually appealing ads (image or video) and target specific audiences based on interests, behavior, and demographics. Instagram allows advertisers to utilize features like stories ads, shoppable posts, and influencer collaborations for effective marketing.

Twitter: Twitter's advertising platform enables businesses to promote their products or services using promoted tweets, trends, and accounts. Targeting options include demographics, interests, and keywords. Advertisers can engage with their audience through various ad formats, including text, image, video, and carousel ads.

LinkedIn: Known as the professional networking platform, LinkedIn offers advertising options focused on B2B marketing.

Advertisers can target specific professional demographics, such as job title, industry, or company size, to reach their desired audience. LinkedIn provides various ad formats, including sponsored content (text and video ads), sponsored InMail, and display ads.

Pinterest: Pinterest is a visual discovery platform with a strong focus on inspiration and shopping. Advertisers can create promoted pins, which appear in users' feeds or search results. Targeting options include interests, keywords, and demographics. Pinterest also offers shopping ads, allowing businesses to showcase their products and direct users to their websites for purchase.

Snapchat: Popular among younger demographics, Snapchat provides advertising options through various ad formats like snap ads (full-screen vertical videos), collection ads, story ads, and augmented reality (AR) lenses. Advertisers can target users based on demographics, interests, and location.

TikTok: TikTok has gained immense popularity with its short-form video content. Businesses can leverage TikTok's advertising platform to create engaging video ads that align with the platform's creative and entertainment-focused nature. Advertisers can target users based on demographics, interests, and behavior.

It's important to note that each platform has its unique user base and advertising features, and choosing the right platform for your business depends on your target audience and marketing objectives.

Demographic and Behavioral Targeting Options

Social media advertising offers a range of demographic and behavioral targeting options to help you reach your desired audience effectively.

Here are some common targeting options:

Demographic Targeting: Platforms allow you to target users based on factors such as age, gender, location, language, education, and income. This helps you narrow down your audience based on specific characteristics.

Interest and Behavior Targeting: This option lets you target users based on their interests, hobbies, online behavior, and past engagement on social media platforms. It helps you find users who are likely to be interested in your product or service.

Custom Audiences: Many platforms provide the ability to create custom audiences using your own customer data, such as email lists or website visitors. This allows you to target specific individuals who have already shown interest in your brand.

Lookalike Audiences: Platforms like Facebook offer the option to create lookalike audiences, where the platform finds users who share similar characteristics to your existing customers. This helps you expand your reach to a larger group of potential customers.

Retargeting: Retargeting allows you to show ads to users who have previously interacted with your brand, such as visitors to your website or viewers of your social media content. This helps you stay top of mind and encourage conversion.

Life Events Targeting: Some platforms offer targeting options based on life events like birthdays, anniversaries, or upcoming weddings. This allows you to tailor your ads to specific moments in users' lives.

When using these targeting options, it's essential to align them with your marketing goals and ensure they comply with privacy regulations. Regularly monitor and analyze campaign performance to optimize your targeting strategy and maximize your results.

By utilizing these advanced targeting options, you can effectively reach the right audience at the right time. Targeting specific individuals who have already shown interest in your brand allows you to focus your efforts on those most likely to convert into customers. This not only saves you valuable time and resources but also increases the chances of generating higher returns on investment.

The power of lookalike audiences should not be underestimated. By leveraging platforms like Facebook, which has a vast user base, you can tap into a pool of potential customers who share similar characteristics with your existing customer base. This means that even if they haven't interacted with your brand yet, there's a high probability that they will be interested in what you have to offer.

Retargeting is another powerful tool in your arsenal. It enables you to stay top-of-mind for users who have previously engaged with your brand but may not have made a purchase or converted yet. By strategically placing ads across various channels such as websites or social media platforms frequented by these users, you increase the likelihood of them returning and completing their desired action - whether it's making a purchase or signing up for a newsletter.

Life events targeting takes personalization one step further by allowing advertisers to tailor their messages based on significant moments in users' lives. Birthdays, anniversaries, weddings - these are all occasions where people are more likely to spend money and make purchasing decisions related to gifts or celebrations. By aligning targeted ads specifically around these life events using relevant keywords or imagery associated with them, businesses can capture consumers' attention during crucial decision-making periods.

However powerful these tools may be when used correctly; it is essential always adhere strictly comply privacy regulations while collecting data from individuals online ensure consumer trust remains intact maintain ethical practices within digital marketing campaigns.

To optimize campaign performance continuously monitor analyze key metrics regularly refine strategies accordingly adapt changing market trends capitalize opportunities arise maximizing your return on investment.

By leveraging advanced targeting options such as lookalike audiences, retargeting, and life events targeting you can effectively reach the right audience at the right time. These tools provide an opportunity to expand your brand's reach while staying top-of-mind with potential customers.

Remember to align these strategies with your marketing goals and comply with privacy regulations to ensure ethical practices are maintained. Continuously monitor campaign performance and adapt accordingly for maximum results in today's competitive digital landscape.

Key Metrics to Measure Advertising Success on Social Media

When it comes to measuring advertising success on social media, there are several key metrics that can provide valuable insights.

Here are a few important ones to consider:

Reach: This metric measures the number of people who have been exposed to your ad. It helps gauge the overall visibility and potential audience that your ad has reached.

Engagement: Engagement metrics, such as likes, comments, shares, and click-through rates, indicate the level of interaction and interest generated by your ad. This metric reflects the effectiveness of your content in capturing and retaining audience attention.

Conversions: Tracking conversions is crucial for determining the return on investment (ROI) of your ads. Whether it's sales, sign-ups, downloads, or any other desired action, this metric reveals how many users have successfully completed the desired action after engaging with your ad.

Cost per Acquisition (CPA): This metric calculates the average cost incurred to acquire a new customer or lead through your ad campaign. Knowing your CPA helps you optimize your budget and assess the efficiency of your advertising efforts.

Return on Ad Spend (ROAS): ROAS measures how much revenue is generated for every dollar spent on advertising. It provides a clear understanding of the overall profitability and effectiveness of your advertising campaigns.

Click-Through Rate (CTR): CTR measures the percentage of people who clicked on your ad after viewing it. A higher CTR often indicates that your ad is compelling and resonating with your target audience.

Brand Awareness: Measuring brand awareness can be done through surveys, social listening tools, and monitoring social media mentions. It helps assess the impact your advertising has had on improving brand recognition and recall.

Remember, the most relevant metrics will vary based on your specific advertising goals and objectives. Make sure to align your measurement strategy with your overall marketing objectives to accurately evaluate the success of your social media advertising campaigns.

CHAPTER 2: CREATING A WINNING ADVERTISING STRATEGY

When it comes to social media advertising, defining clear goals and objectives is essential for a successful campaign.

Here are some key steps to help you do just that:

Identify your target audience: Before setting goals, it's crucial to understand who you want to reach with your social media ads. Define your target audience based on demographics, interests, and behaviors.

Determine your advertising goals: Your goals should align with your overall marketing objectives. Common social media advertising goals include increasing brand awareness, driving website traffic, expanding reach, generating leads, or boosting sales.

Set measurable objectives: Once you've identified your goals, set specific, measurable, achievable, relevant, and time-bound (SMART) objectives. For example, aim to increase website traffic by 20% within three months or generate 100 new leads in a month.

Consider key performance indicators (KPIs): To track your progress, identify KPIs that are relevant to your goals. KPIs can include metrics like click-through rates, engagement rates, conversion rates, cost per acquisition, or return on ad spend.

Create compelling ad content: Develop engaging and visually appealing ad content that resonates with your target audience. Consider using high-quality images or videos, compelling copy, and strong call-to-action statements.

Choose the right social media platforms: Select the social media platforms that align with your target audience and advertising goals. Each platform has its own strengths and demographics, so conduct research to determine where your audience is most active.

Track and analyze campaign performance: Regularly monitor the performance of your social media ads using analytics tools provided by the platforms or third-party tools. Analyze data to make data-driven decisions and optimize your campaigns for better results.

Remember, goals and objectives for social media advertising can vary depending on your business and industry. It's essential to regularly review and adapt your strategies based on the campaign results and evolving consumer behaviors.

Identifying Target Audience and Creating Buyer Personas

When it comes to social media advertising, identifying your target audience and creating buyer personas is crucial for effective targeting and messaging.

Here's how you can go about it:

Research: Start by researching your existing customers or target market. Look into demographics, interests, behaviors, and preferences. Use tools like Google Analytics, social media insights, and customer surveys to gather data.

Segmentation: Break down your audience into segments based on common characteristics such as age, location, gender, occupation, and lifestyle.

Develop Buyer Personas: Once you have segmented your audience, create detailed buyer personas that represent your ideal customers. These personas should include demographics, goals, challenges, motivations, and media consumption habits.

Define Persona Attributes: Assign specific attributes to your buyer personas, such as a name, age, occupation, family status, hobbies, and key pain points they may experience.

Understand Motivations: Dive deeper into your personas' motivations and needs. What drives them to make a purchase? What problem are they trying to solve? How can your product or service help them?

Craft Messaging: With your buyer personas in mind, tailor your social media advertising messaging to speak directly to their needs and desires. Use language and visuals that resonate with each persona.

Targeting: Utilize the targeting capabilities of social media advertising platforms to reach your identified buyer personas. Narrow down your audience based on demographics, interests, behaviors, and location.

Test and Optimize: Continuously monitor the performance of your social media ads and make adjustments to improve effectiveness. Split testing different creatives, ad placements, and messaging can help optimize your campaigns.

The key to successful social media advertising lies in consistently refining your target audience and buyer personas based on data and feedback. Regularly reassess and update your personas to keep up with changing trends and customer preferences.

Creating engaging ad campaigns for social media advertising involves careful planning and strategic content creation.

Here are some steps to help you in the process:

Define your objectives: Clearly identify your goals for the ad campaign. Are you looking to increase brand awareness, drive website traffic, generate leads, or promote a specific product or service?

Know your target audience: Research and analyze your target audience to understand their demographics, interests, and behaviors. This will help you create relevant and engaging content that resonates with them.

Choose the right social media platforms: Determine which social media platforms align with your target audience and are most effective for achieving your objectives. Each platform has its own unique features and strengths.

Develop your content strategy: Create a content plan that includes key messaging, visuals, and a consistent brand voice. Consider incorporating storytelling, user-generated content, and interactive elements to make your ads more engaging.

Use compelling visuals: Invest in high-quality visuals, such as images and videos, that capture attention and convey your message effectively. Utilize eye-catching designs, bold colors, and attention-grabbing headlines to stand out in social media feeds.

Test and optimize: A/B test different ad variations to determine which perform best. Monitor the metrics and make data-driven decisions to optimize your campaigns over time. This will help you continually improve and achieve better results.

Leverage user-generated content: Encourage your audience to create and share content related to your brand. This not only increases engagement but also builds trust and authenticity around your products or services.

Implement a call-to-action: Clearly define the action you want your audience to take, whether it's visiting your website, making a purchase, or signing up for a newsletter. Include a strong and persuasive call-to-action in your ad copy.

Monitor and analyze results: Regularly track the performance of your ad campaigns using social media analytics tools. Evaluate key metrics, such as click-through rates, conversion rates, engagement, and ROI. Adjust your strategy based on the findings to maximize your success.

Creating engaging ad campaigns requires a deep understanding of your target audience, strategic planning, and continuous optimization. By following these steps, you can effectively reach and engage your audience on social media platforms.

Setting a Budget and Allocating Resources Effectively

Setting a budget and allocating resources effectively for social media advertising is crucial for achieving desired results without overspending.

Here are some steps to help you navigate this process:

Define your goals: Clearly outline your objectives for social media advertising. Whether it's increasing brand awareness, driving website traffic, or generating leads, having specific goals will guide your budget decisions.

Analyze your target audience: Understand your target audience's demographics, interests, and online behavior. This analysis will help you choose the most effective social media platforms to invest in and allocate your budget accordingly.

Research advertising costs: Different social media platforms have varying advertising costs. Research and compare the pricing structures, such as cost per click (CPC) or cost per thousand impressions (CPM), to determine which channels align with your budget.

Determine your budget: Assess your financial resources and set a realistic budget for social media advertising. Consider factors like the size of your target audience, campaign duration, and desired reach. Remember to leave room for testing and adjustments along the way.

Test and optimize: Start by allocating a smaller portion of your budget to test different ad formats, targeting options, and messaging strategies. Monitor the performance of these ads closely and optimize them based on the data you gather. This iterative approach helps you maximize the effectiveness of your budget allocation.

Utilize targeting options: Take advantage of the advanced targeting options offered by social media platforms. Refine your audience selection based on criteria like location, age, interests, and behaviors. The more targeted your ads, the better the chance of reaching the right people within your budget.

Monitor and track performance: Continuously monitor your ad campaigns' performance using analytics provided by the platforms. Identify what's working and what's not and make data-driven adjustments accordingly. This helps you optimize your resources and allocate budget to the most effective ads.

Experiment and learn: Social media advertising is not a one-size-fits-all approach, so be open to experimentation. Try different ad formats, visuals, CTAs, and copy variations to identify what resonates best with your audience. Learn from each campaign to inform your future budget allocations.

Remember, successful budget allocation for social media advertising requires a combination of strategic planning, ongoing optimization, and a willingness to adapt based on data-driven insights. By following these steps, you can make the most of your resources and achieve desired results.

CHAPTER 3: CHOOSING THE RIGHT SOCIAL MEDIA CHANNELS

Comparing Major Social Media Platforms (Facebook, Instagram, Twitter, LinkedIn, etc.)

When comparing major social media platforms like Facebook, Instagram, Twitter, LinkedIn, and others, it's important to consider their unique features, target audience, and primary uses.

Here's an overview:

Facebook: As one of the most popular social media platforms, Facebook caters to a broad range of users. It emphasizes personal connections, allowing users to share updates, photos, videos, and interact with friends and family. Its News Feed algorithm prioritizes content based on user preferences.

Instagram: Focusing on visual content, Instagram is widely used for sharing photos and videos. It appeals to a younger demographic and offers features like filters, stories, and IGTV. Instagram also enables users to follow accounts based on interests, discover content through hashtags, and engage with influencers.

Twitter: Known for its real-time updates and concise nature, Twitter allows users to post short text messages (called tweets) limited to 280 characters. It serves as a platform for news, discussions, and conversations on various topics. Twitter emphasizes following other users and utilizes hashtags for content discovery and trending topics.

LinkedIn: Geared towards professionals and networking, LinkedIn provides a platform for users to showcase their skills, education, and work experience. It fosters professional connections, job searching, and industry discussions. LinkedIn encourages users to build a strong professional presence and engage with relevant content.

While these are just a few examples, each platform has its own unique strengths and purposes. Understanding the target audience and key features of social media platforms can help determine the most suitable platform for specific needs, whether it's personal connections, visual content sharing, breaking news, or professional networking.

Analyzing Platform Demographics and User Engagement

To analyze platform demographics and user engagement for social media advertising, there are several steps you can follow:

Identify the platforms: Determine which social media platforms you are interested in analyzing. The most popular ones include Facebook, Instagram, Twitter, LinkedIn, and Snapchat.

Source demographic data: Gather demographic information about the platforms you have chosen. This data can often be found through the platforms' own advertising tools, third-party research reports, or industry publications. Look for details such as age, gender, location, income level, and interests.

Analyze user engagement metrics: Examine user engagement metrics specific to each platform. These may include metrics like likes, comments, shares, retweets, and click-through rates. Platforms usually provide analytics tools or insights that allow you to monitor such engagement metrics.

Compare engagement across platforms: Compare the engagement metrics across different platforms to understand which ones are more effective for your target audience. Look for patterns and trends, such as higher engagement among certain demographic groups or in specific types of content (e.g., images, videos, articles).

Consider ad formats: Evaluate the ad formats available on each platform and their effectiveness in capturing user attention. Some platforms offer various formats like image ads, carousel ads, video ads, or sponsored content. Look for insights or case studies that can help you determine the best formats for your advertising goals.

Utilize audience targeting options: Explore the targeting options offered by each platform. These typically allow you to specify the characteristics of your desired audience, such as age, location, interests, and behaviors. Understanding the targeting capabilities of each platform will help you reach your desired audience more effectively.

Monitor industry trends: Stay updated on the latest industry trends and changes in social media platforms. This will help you adapt your advertising strategies accordingly and potentially benefit from new features or functionalities.

By following these steps, you can gain a better understanding of the demographics and user engagement on various social media platforms, allowing you to make informed decisions when planning and executing your social media advertising campaigns.

Determining Which Platforms Align with
Advertising Goals and Target Audience

When it comes to determining which platforms align with your advertising goals and target audience for social media advertising, there are a few key factors to consider.

First, identify your advertising goals. Are you looking to increase brand awareness, generate leads, drive sales, or promote a specific product or service? Different platforms have different strengths and capabilities, so aligning your goals with the platform's strengths is crucial.

Next, understand your target audience. Who are they? What demographics do they fall into, such as age, gender, location, and interests? Each social media platform attracts a different user base, so selecting the platforms that are most popular among your target audience will increase the effectiveness of your advertising efforts.

To help you make an informed decision, here's a breakdown of the major social media platforms and their key characteristics:

Facebook: With over 2.7 billion monthly active users, Facebook offers a vast reach and extensive targeting options. It is suitable for various goals and has a diverse user base covering a wide range of demographics.

Instagram: Known for its visual content, Instagram is popular among younger audiences, particularly millennials and Gen Z. It is effective for showcasing products or services that have a strong visual appeal.

Twitter: Twitter is ideal for real-time engagement, news updates, and promoting timely content. It has a slightly older user base and is often used by professionals and those seeking quick, concise information.

LinkedIn: Consider LinkedIn if your target audience consists of professionals, B2B businesses, or if you are looking to hire talent. Its focus is on networking and business-related content.

Pinterest: Popular for lifestyle, DIY, and design inspiration, Pinterest has a primarily female user base. If your product or service fits into these categories, Pinterest can be a valuable platform to reach your target audience.

TikTok: TikTok is gaining popularity among younger audiences, especially Gen Z. Its short-form video format makes it ideal for creative and entertaining content.

Remember to analyze the analytics and performance metrics provided by each platform to track the effectiveness of your advertising efforts. Experimentation and monitoring results will help you refine your approach and maximize your return on investment.

CHAPTER 4: CRAFTING COMPELLING ADVERTISEMENTS

Elements of Effective Social Media Ad Copy

When it comes to creating effective social media ad copy, there are several key elements to consider.

Here are some important factors to keep in mind:

Attention-Grabbing Headline: Your ad copy should have a compelling headline that grabs the reader's attention and entices them to continue reading. Use strong and impactful language to make your headline stand out.

Clear and Concise Message: Keep your message straightforward and concise. Avoid jargon or complicated language that might confuse your audience. Clearly communicate the purpose of your ad and what you are offering.

Value Proposition: Highlight the unique value or benefits your product or service provides. Explain how it can solve a problem or fulfill a need for your target audience. Make sure to use persuasive language to convince readers that engaging with your ad is worth their time.

Call-to-Action: Include a clear call-to-action (CTA) that tells the reader what action you want them to take. Use action-oriented verbs and create a sense of urgency to encourage immediate response.

Visual Appeal: Pair your ad copy with visually appealing graphics or images that align with your message. Strong visuals can capture attention and enhance the impact of your ad.

Targeted Language and Tone: Tailor your ad copy to your specific audience. Consider their demographics, interests, and pain points. Craft your message in a tone that resonates with them and sparks their interest.

Test and Optimize: As with any marketing strategy, it's crucial to test different variations of your ad copy to see what resonates best with your audience. Continuously monitor and analyze the performance of your ads and adjust accordingly.

By incorporating these elements into your social media ad copy, you can increase the effectiveness of your campaigns and better engage your target audience.

Designing Visually Appealing Ads That Stand Out

When it comes to designing visually appealing ads for social media advertising, there are several key elements and strategies to keep in mind. By following these guidelines, you can create ads that stand out and catch the attention of your target audience.

Understand your target audience: Before designing your ads, it's important to have a clear understanding of who you are trying to reach. Research their demographics, interests, and preferences to tailor your ad design accordingly.

Use eye-catching visuals: Visuals are a crucial aspect of social media ads. Choose high-quality images or videos that are relevant to your message and visually engaging. Make sure they are clear, colorful, and visually appealing to capture attention as users scroll through their feeds.

Keep it simple and focused: Don't overwhelm your audience with too much information. Keep your message concise and focused to make it easier for viewers to absorb. Use attention-grabbing headlines and key points to convey your message effectively.

Incorporate branding elements: Maintain consistency with your brand's visual identity. Use your logo, colors, and fonts in your ad design to ensure brand recognition. However, avoid overcrowding the ad with branding elements, as it may distract from the main message.

Follow platform guidelines: Each social media platform has specific guidelines for ad dimensions and formats. Adhere to these guidelines to ensure your ads are displayed correctly and look professional on the platform.

Use compelling copy: Pair your visuals with persuasive and concise copy. Craft a compelling headline and tagline that grabs attention and entices users to take action. Keep the text short and to the point, as users typically have limited attention spans.

Test and iterate: Don't be afraid to experiment with different ad designs. Test multiple versions of your ads to see what resonates best with your audience. Analyze the performance metrics and adjust accordingly to optimize your ads over time.

Remember, the key to designing visually appealing ads for social media is to engage your target audience, deliver a clear message, and align with your brand identity. By implementing these strategies, you can create ads that stand out and drive results.

Incorporating Persuasive Calls-to-Action

Are you looking to boost engagement and drive conversions through social media advertising? Look no further! With carefully crafted persuasive calls-to-action (CTAs), you can inspire your audience to take the desired actions.

Here are a few helpful tips to help you incorporate effective CTAs into your social media ads:

Be clear and concise: Keep your CTA short and sweet, making it easy for your audience to understand and act upon. Avoid confusing language or jargon that might cause hesitation or uncertainty.

Use action verbs: Encourage immediate action by incorporating strong action verbs in your CTA. Words like "shop now," "learn more," or "join today" can compel users to take the desired action.

Create a sense of urgency: Instill a sense of urgency to create a fear of missing out (FOMO) among your audience. Phrases like "limited time offer" or "sale ends soon" can motivate users to act quickly to avoid missing out on a great opportunity.

Offer incentives: People love getting something in return for their actions. Consider providing a special offer, discount, or freebie alongside your CTA to further entice your audience. Phrases like "get 15% off today" or "download our free e-book" can greatly increase click-through rates.

Customize for each platform: Tailor your CTAs to fit the specific social media platform you're using. For example, on Instagram, you can make use of the "swipe up" feature in Stories to direct users to a landing page. On Facebook, you can utilize their built-in CTA buttons to guide users to take action.

Test and optimize: Don't be afraid to experiment with different CTAs to see what works best for your audience. A/B testing can help you identify the most effective words, phrases, or design elements that drive the highest engagement and conversions.

Remember, the key to a persuasive CTA is to create a sense of urgency, offer clear benefits, and make it easy for users to take action. By implementing these tips, you'll be well on your way to crafting compelling CTAs that drive results in your social media advertising campaigns. So go ahead, inspire your audience, and watch your conversions soar!

When it comes to A/B testing and optimizing ad performance for social media advertising, there are a few key steps you can follow to help achieve better results.

Define clear objectives: Start by identifying your goals and what you want to achieve with your social media ads. Whether it's increasing brand awareness, driving website traffic, or generating leads, having clear objectives will guide your testing and optimization efforts.

Create multiple ad variations: Develop different versions of your ads by changing elements such as headlines, images, ad copy, and calls-to-action. This allows you to test different variables and determine which combination resonates best with your audience.

Split your audience: Divide your target audience into groups, ensuring each group is exposed to a different ad variation. Make sure the groups are of sufficient size to produce statistically valid results.

Monitor and measure results: Track key metrics like click-through rates (CTR), conversion rates, engagement levels, and cost-per-acquisition. Use analytics tools provided by social media platforms to gather data and assess performance.

Analyze and interpret data: Compare the performance of your different ad variations and identify patterns or trends. Look for insights on what elements or combinations are driving better outcomes.

Make data-driven decisions: Based on the insights gained, choose the winning ad variation, and allocate more budget towards it. Consider making incremental changes to optimize further, such as tweaking ad copy or testing different target audiences.

Continually test and optimize: A/B testing is an iterative process.

Keep refining your ads, conduct ongoing experiments, and adapt to changes in your audience's preferences or market dynamics.

Remember, A/B testing is not a one-time effort but rather a continuous practice to improve the effectiveness of your social media ads. Regularly revisiting ad performance and implementing optimizations will help you achieve your advertising goals more efficiently.

CHAPTER 5: LEVERAGING AD TARGETING AND REMARKETING

Utilizing Demographic, Interest, and Behavioral Targeting Options

Social media advertising offers a wealth of targeting options to help businesses effectively reach their desired audience. Demographic targeting allows you to reach users based on specific characteristics such as age, gender, location, and language. This helps you to tailor your ads to the right people and maximize their relevancy.

Interest targeting enables you to reach individuals who have shown an interest in particular topics, activities, or hobbies. By understanding users' interests, you can create ads that resonate with them and increase the likelihood of engagement and conversion.

Behavioral targeting allows you to target users based on their online behaviors and activities. This includes factors such as past purchasing behavior, website visits, app usage, and more. By analyzing user behavior, you can create highly targeted ads that are more likely to convert.

To make the most of these targeting options, it's important to:

Define your target audience: Clearly identify your ideal customer persona based on demographic, interest, and behavioral traits.

Set specific campaign goals: Determine what actions you want users to take (e.g., website visits, app downloads, purchases) to focus your targeting efforts.

Utilize platform-specific targeting features: Each social media platform has its own targeting options and tools. Familiarize yourself with them and use them effectively.

Test and optimize: Monitor the performance of your ads and make adjustments as needed. Continuously test different targeting options to find what works best for your audience.

By leveraging demographic, interest, and behavioral targeting options, you can refine your social media advertising strategy and efficiently reach your desired audience, increasing the chances of driving meaningful results for your business.

Implementing Audience Segmentation Strategies

Audience segmentation strategies are crucial for effective social media advertising. By targeting specific groups of users based on their demographics, behaviors, and interests, you can optimize your ad campaigns and achieve better results.

Here's a step-by-step guide for implementing audience segmentation strategies for social media advertising:

Define your objectives: Start by clearly defining your advertising objectives. Are you looking to increase brand awareness, drive website traffic, generate leads, or boost sales? This will help you determine which audience segments to prioritize.

Identify relevant demographics: Analyze your target audience and identify key demographic characteristics such as age, gender, location, income level, and education. This will help you create segments based on these factors.

Analyze user behavior and interests: Social media platforms provide valuable insights into user behavior and interests. Use these insights to identify common patterns, preferences, and interests among your target audience. This information can be used to create segments based on user behavior, such as frequent online shoppers or tech enthusiasts.

Utilize psychographic segmentation: Psychographic segmentation considers users' values, personality traits, attitudes, and lifestyles. It provides deeper insights into consumer motivations and preferences. Leverage psychographic data to create segments based on common interests, values, or lifestyle choices.

Use custom and lookalike audiences: Custom audiences allow you to upload customer data, such as email lists or website visitors, to create highly targeted segments. Lookalike audiences, on the other hand, help you reach new users who are similar to your existing customers. Utilize these features to expand your reach while targeting specific segments.

Test and refine: Continuously monitor the performance of your ad campaigns using analytics tools provided by social media platforms. Analyze key metrics like click-through rates, conversions, and engagement to identify which segments are responding best to your ads. Make adjustments as needed to optimize your campaigns.

Personalize ad content: Tailor your ad content to each segment, addressing their specific needs, pain points, and preferences. This personalization will increase the relevance and effectiveness of your ads, leading to higher engagement and conversions.

Remember, audience segmentation is an ongoing process. Continuously update and refine your segments based on user behavior and campaign performance to ensure the best results.

Retargeting website visitors is a valuable strategy to boost conversions in social media advertising. By reaching out to users who have already shown interest in your website, you can increase the likelihood of them completing a purchase or taking desired action.

Here's how to effectively implement retargeting for improved conversions:

Install a tracking pixel: Begin by placing a retargeting pixel on your website. This snippet of code tracks visitors and allows you to target them later on social media platforms.

Define your audience segments: Determine specific audience segments based on user behavior, such as people who abandoned their shopping carts or those who browsed specific product pages. Segmenting your audience helps deliver more personalized ads.

Craft compelling ad content: Create visually appealing and persuasive ads that align with your audience segments. Use enticing images, compelling copy, and a clear call-to-action to encourage users to take the desired action.

Utilize dynamic retargeting: Dynamic retargeting involves showing users ads featuring products or services they have already viewed. This personalized approach can significantly increase conversion rates, as it reminds users of products, they were interested in.

Frequency capping: Be mindful of frequency capping, which limits how often users see your retargeting ads. This prevents ad fatigue and annoyance, helping to maintain positive user experience.

Test and optimize: Continuously monitor your retargeting campaigns and optimize them based on performance. Experiment with different ad formats, messaging, and audience segments to find what works best for your business.

Cross-platform retargeting: Expand your retargeting efforts beyond social media platforms by utilizing other channels like email marketing and display advertising. This multi-channel approach can reinforce your message and further increase conversions.

By employing these strategies, you can harness the power of retargeting to increase conversions for your social media advertising efforts. Remember to analyze data, adapt your tactics, and always strive for continuous improvement.

Custom Audience Creation and Lookalike Audience Targeting

Custom audience creation and lookalike audience targeting are powerful tools for social media advertising.

Custom audience creation allows you to reach specific groups of individuals who have already shown interest in your business. For example, you can target existing customers, website visitors, or people who have engaged with your social media content. This ensures that your ads are served to a more relevant audience, increasing the chances of driving conversions.

Lookalike audience targeting takes custom audience creation a step further by finding new people who share similar characteristics to your existing audience. This helps you expand your reach and target individuals who are more likely to be interested in your products or services.

To create a custom audience, you can upload a customer list, use website tracking pixels, or leverage engagement data from social media platforms. Once your custom audience is created, you can fine-tune your targeting by adding additional parameters like demographics or interests.

For lookalike audience targeting, you need to have a custom audience as a base. The social media platform then uses algorithms to find people who have similar attributes to your custom audience. This can be an effective way to reach new potential customers with highly targeted ads.

Both custom audience creation and lookalike audience targeting can significantly improve the effectiveness of your social media advertising campaigns. By delivering your ads to a more relevant and interested audience, you can increase engagement, drive more conversions, and achieve better ROI.

CHAPTER 6: MANAGING AND OPTIMIZING CAMPAIGNS

Implementing Effective Campaign Tracking
and Measurement Strategies

When it comes to implementing effective campaign tracking and measurement strategies for social media advertising, there are a few key steps you can follow to ensure accurate data collection and meaningful insights.

Here's what you can do:

Set clear campaign objectives: Before launching any campaign, define specific and measurable objectives. Whether it's increasing brand awareness, driving website traffic, or generating leads, having clear goals will help you track and measure the right metrics.

Use UTM parameters: Implement UTM (Urchin Tracking Module) parameters in your campaign URLs. UTM parameters allow you to track the source, medium, and campaign names in your website analytics tools. This provides valuable insights into the effectiveness of your social media advertising efforts.

Leverage conversion tracking: Set up conversion tracking pixels or tags on your website to track user actions such as form submissions, purchases, or newsletter sign-ups. Most social media advertising platforms provide these tracking options, which allow you to measure the ROI of your campaigns accurately.

Utilize social media analytics tools: Take advantage of the analytics tools provided by social media platforms. Platforms like Facebook, Instagram, and Twitter offer detailed insights into campaign reach, engagement, and conversion metrics. Regularly review and analyze these metrics to assess the performance of your campaigns.

Establish KPIs: Identify key performance indicators (KPIs) that align with your campaign objectives. These could include metrics like click-through rate (CTR), conversion rate, cost per acquisition (CPA), or return on ad spend (ROAS). Tracking KPIs will help you monitor and optimize the effectiveness of your social media advertising campaigns.

A/B testing: Conduct A/B tests by running multiple variations of your ads simultaneously. Test different ad creatives, messaging, targeting options, or call-to-actions to identify the best performing elements. A/B testing enables data-driven decision making and helps optimize campaign performance.

Regular reporting and analysis: Establish a reporting schedule to track the performance of your campaigns consistently. Create easy-to-understand reports that highlight the key metrics and insights. Regular analysis of campaign data will enable you to make data-driven optimizations and improve future social media advertising efforts.

Remember, effective campaign tracking and measurement strategies are an ongoing process. Continuously monitoring, analyzing, and refining your campaigns based on insights will help maximize the return on your social media advertising investment.

When it comes to analyzing campaign performance metrics for social media advertising, there are a few key steps to follow:

Set clear objectives: Before diving into data analysis, establish specific goals for your social media campaign. These could include increasing brand awareness, driving website traffic, or generating leads.

Identify relevant metrics: Determine which metrics are most important for tracking the success of your campaign. Common metrics include impressions, reach, engagement (likes, comments, shares), click-through rates (CTR), conversion rates, and return on ad spend (ROAS).

Gather data from your social media platforms: Use the analytics tools provided by each platform (such as Facebook Insights or Twitter Analytics) to collect data on your campaign's performance. Pay attention to key metrics and any patterns or trends you observe.

Analyze the data: Dive into the numbers and look for insights. Identify which posts or ads performed well and which did not. Compare different metrics to gain a comprehensive understanding of your campaign's effectiveness. Look for any correlations or factors that may have influenced the outcomes.

Adjust your strategies: Based on the analysis of your campaign's performance, make data-driven decisions to optimize your strategies. Consider adjusting your target audience, messaging, visuals, or ad placements to maximize results. Experiment with different techniques and measure the impact of these changes on your metrics.

Test and iterate: Social media advertising is a dynamic environment, so it's important to continuously test and iterate your strategies. Monitor the impact of any adjustments you make and be ready to adapt based on the results you observe.

By following these steps, you'll be able to effectively analyze campaign performance metrics for your social media advertising and make informed decisions to optimize your strategies.

Split Testing Ad Variations for Optimal Results

Split testing ad variations is a crucial practice to optimize results in social media advertising.

Here are some steps to help you run effective split tests:

Define your objectives: Clearly identify what you want to achieve with your ad campaign, whether it's increasing brand awareness, driving website traffic, or generating leads. This will help you set measurable goals.

Identify variables: Determine the elements of your ads that you want to test. It could be the headline, ad copy, call-to-action, visual elements, or targeting options. Make sure to test one variable at a time to accurately measure its impact.

Create ad variations: Develop multiple versions of your ad, each with a different variable than that you're testing. Ensure that each variation is distinct and measurable, enabling you to identify which one performs better.

Set up the split test: Use the ad platform's built-in split testing feature or an external tool to evenly distribute your ad variations to your target audience. It's important to ensure that the test is deployed randomly and reaches a statistically significant sample size.

Monitor and measure results: Track the performance of each ad variation by monitoring key metrics such as click-through rates, conversion rates, cost per result, and return on ad spend. Collect enough data to confidently determine the winning ad variation.

Declare a winner: Once enough data has been collected, compare the performance of your ad variations, and declare a winner based on your predefined objectives. The winning variation becomes your control for future tests.

Iterate and optimize: Take the insights gained from your split test and apply them to future ad campaigns. Test new variables and continue refining your approach to achieve better results over time.

Remember, split testing is an ongoing process that requires continuous experimentation and optimization to maximize the effectiveness of your social media advertising.

Leveraging Data-Driven Insights to Refine Targeting and Messaging

Data-driven insights are invaluable when it comes to refining targeting and messaging strategies. By harnessing the power of data, businesses can better understand their target audience, make informed decisions, and create more effective marketing campaigns.

Here's how you can leverage data-driven insights to refine targeting and messaging:

Identify key metrics: Start by identifying the key metrics that align with your business goals, such as conversion rates, click-through rates, or customer lifetime value. These metrics will serve as a foundation for analyzing data and measuring the success of your targeting and messaging efforts.

Collect relevant data: Gather data from various sources, such as website analytics, social media platforms, customer surveys, or sales records. Ensure that you have a robust data collection system in place to capture both demographic and behavioral information about your target audience.

Analyze and segment your audience: Analyze the collected data to identify patterns, trends, and segments within your target audience. Look for common characteristics, preferences, or behaviors that can help you tailor your messaging and targeting efforts more effectively.

Personalize messaging: Use the gathered insights to create personalized messaging that resonates with different audience segments. Craft your content in a way that addresses their specific pain points, desires, or interests. Personalization can significantly enhance engagement and conversion rates.

Test and optimize: Continuously monitor and test your messaging and targeting strategies using A/B testing or other experimentation techniques. Gather feedback, measure results, and make data-driven adjustments to improve your campaigns over time.

Automate where possible: Leverage automation tools and platforms to streamline your targeting and messaging processes. Automation can help you scale your efforts, segment your audience more accurately, and deliver personalized content at the right time and through the most effective channels.

Remember, data-driven insights are only valuable when you use them to inform your decision-making and take action. Stay agile, adapt your strategies based on the data, and always strive for continuous improvement.

CHAPTER 7: MAXIMIZING ROI AND CONVERSION RATES

Strategies for Increasing Click-Through Rates and Engagement

Increasing click-through rates and engagement is crucial for any business or online platform.

Here are some effective strategies to achieve this:

Compelling Headlines: Craft attention-grabbing headlines that spark curiosity and make readers want to click. Use words like "exclusive," "ultimate," or ask intriguing questions.

Quality Content: Offer valuable and well-researched content that resonates with your target audience. This will establish trust and encourage users to engage further.

Visual Appeal: Incorporate eye-catching visuals such as images, videos, or infographics to enhance the attractiveness of your content. Visuals can significantly increase engagement and persuade users to click.

Clear Call-to-Action (CTA): Use clear and concise CTAs that guide users towards the desired action. Utilize action-oriented verbs and place the CTA in a prominent position on your page or website.

Personalization: Tailor your content to address the specific interests and needs of your audience. Personalization creates a sense of relevance and increases the likelihood of click-throughs and engagement.

Mobile Optimization: Ensure that your website or content is optimized for mobile devices. With the majority of users accessing content through smartphones, a mobile-friendly experience is crucial for increasing engagement and click-through rates.

Split Testing: Conduct A/B testing on various elements such as headlines, images, CTAs, and content formats to determine what resonates best with your audience. This allows you to refine your approach and maximize engagement.

Social Proof: Incorporate social proof elements such as user reviews, testimonials, or social media shares to build trust and credibility. Seeing positive feedback from others can encourage users to engage with your content or click through.

Influencer Collaboration: Partner with relevant influencers or industry experts to promote your content or offerings. Their endorsement can significantly increase click-through rates and engagement among their followers.

Analyze and Optimize: Regularly analyze your metrics, such as click-through rates, time spent on page, and bounce rates. Identify areas for improvement and make data-driven optimizations to continually enhance engagement.

Remember, building click-through rates and engagement is an ongoing process. By implementing these strategies and consistently reviewing your analytics, you can optimize your approach and achieve better results over time.

Optimizing Landing Pages for Improved Conversions

When it comes to optimizing landing pages for improved conversions, there are several key strategies and best practices to keep in mind.

Here are some actionable tips to help you boost your conversion rates:

Clear and compelling headline: Craft a captivating headline that clearly communicates the value proposition or the benefits your product or service offers. Make it stand out and grab users' attention.

Concise and persuasive copy: Use clear and concise language to explain the key features and benefits of your product or service. Focus on how it solves a problem or fulfills a need for your target audience and avoid using jargon or complex language.

Attention-grabbing visuals: Incorporate relevant and visually appealing images, videos, or graphics that support your message and engage users. Use high-quality visuals that are properly optimized for the web to ensure fast loading times.

Streamlined form design: If your landing page includes a form, keep it simple and only ask for essential information. Long and complicated forms can deter users from completing them. Consider using auto-fill capabilities and reducing the number of required fields.

Strong call-to-action (CTA): Place a clear and prominent CTA button on your landing page that stands out and compels users to take action. Use action-oriented language (e.g., "Get started," "Download now") to prompt users to follow through and convert.

Mobile optimization: Ensure that your landing page is fully optimized for mobile devices, as an increasing number of users browse the internet on their smartphones and tablets. Responsive design and quick loading times are crucial for a positive mobile user experience.

A/B testing: Experiment with different elements on your landing page, such as headlines, copy, visuals, CTAs, and form designs. Conduct A/B tests to compare different variations and identify what resonates best with your target audience. Make data-driven decisions to optimize your page further.

Social proof and testimonials: Incorporate social proof elements, such as customer testimonials, case studies, or reviews, to build trust and credibility. Highlight positive feedback or success stories to reassure visitors and increase their confidence in your offering.

Remember, optimizing landing pages for improved conversions is an ongoing process. Continuously monitor your page's performance, analyze user behavior, and make data-driven optimizations based on your findings.

Implementing Retargeting Campaigns for
Abandoned Carts or Incomplete Actions

Retargeting campaigns can be highly effective in recovering potential customers who have abandoned their carts or not completed desired actions on your website.

Here's how you can implement retargeting campaigns specifically for abandoned carts or incomplete actions:

Set up tracking: Install a tracking pixel or code on your website to identify users who have abandoned their carts or have not completed desired actions. This will allow you to segment and target these specific audiences.

Create compelling ads: Develop visually appealing and attention-grabbing ads that highlight the products or services the user shows interest in. It's important to remind them of the value or benefits they would receive by completing the action.

Use personalized messaging: Tailor your messaging to remind the user about their abandoned cart or incomplete action specifically. Mention the items they left behind or the action they didn't complete and emphasize any incentives such as discounts or limited time offers to encourage them to come back.

Set a frequency cap: Avoid bombarding users with too many retargeting ads. Set a frequency cap to limit how often your ads are shown to prevent annoyance. Showing ads too frequently can have a negative impact on the user's experience and might deter them from returning to complete their action.

Test different ad formats and placements: Experiment with various ad formats (e.g., static images, animated banners, video) and placements (e.g., social media, display networks, email) to determine what works best for your audience. Continuously monitor and optimize your campaigns based on their performance.

Offer incentives or reminders: Consider offering incentives to entice users to return and complete their action, such as free shipping, a coupon code, or a limited-time discount. Additionally, sending automated reminder emails or push notifications can serve as gentle nudges to encourage users to finalize their purchase or fill out forms.

Monitor and optimize: Regularly analyze the performance of your retargeting campaigns. Measure key metrics like click-through rates, conversion rates, and overall ROI. Based on these insights, make necessary adjustments to optimize your campaigns and achieve better results.

Remember, retargeting campaigns are most effective when they provide relevant, personalized content to remind users of their abandoned carts or incomplete actions. By implementing these strategies, you can effectively bring back potential customers and increase your chances of completing desired actions.

Leveraging Social Proof and User-Generated Content to Build Trust

When it comes to building trust with your audience, leveraging social proof and user-generated content can be incredibly effective strategies. Social proof refers to the concept that people are more likely to trust and engage with something if they see that others have already done so. User-generated content, on the other hand, involves encouraging and showcasing content created by your customers or users.

Here's how you can effectively leverage these strategies:

Reviews and testimonials: Display positive reviews and testimonials from satisfied customers on your website, social media platforms, and other marketing materials. Authentic and detailed reviews can provide reassurance to potential customers and help build trust in your brand.

Social media engagement: Encourage your customers to engage with your brand on social media by sharing their experiences, feedback, and photos. This user-generated content not only adds credibility but also creates a sense of community around your brand.

Influencer collaborations: Partnering with influencers in your industry who have a strong following can significantly boost your credibility and trustworthiness. When influencers endorse your products or services, their audience is more likely to trust your brand based on the influencer's reputation.

Case studies: Develop case studies that highlight how your products or services have helped previous customers achieve their goals. By showcasing real-life examples and sharing measurable results, you can demonstrate the value and effectiveness of your offerings.

Social media contests and giveaways: Encourage user-generated content by hosting contests and giveaways that require participants to share their experiences or create content related to your brand. This not only increases engagement but also generates user-generated content that can be shared and leveraged for building trust.

Remember, the key to successfully leveraging social proof and user-generated content is to ensure authenticity and transparency. Avoid fake reviews or fabricated content, as they can quickly damage trust in your brand. Ultimately, by effectively utilizing social proof and user-generated content, you can build a strong foundation of trust with your audience and boost your brand's credibility.

CHAPTER 8: EXPANDING REACH WITH INFLUENCER MARKETING

Understanding the Role of Influencers in Social Media Advertising

Influencers play a significant role in social media advertising. They are individuals who have built a strong following and have the power to influence the thoughts, actions, and purchasing decisions of their audience. These influencers create content that resonates with their followers, aligning their personal brand with the products or services they promote.

One of the key benefits of working with influencers is their ability to reach a specific target audience. By partnering with an influencer whose followers align with a brand's target demographic, companies can effectively promote their products or services to a highly engaged audience.

Influencers also bring authenticity to advertising campaigns. Their followers trust their recommendations because they perceive them as genuine and relatable. This trust translates into higher engagement rates and increased credibility for brands.

Moreover, influencers can provide unique and creative content for brands. Their expertise in creating visually appealing and engaging posts can help companies stand out in a crowded social media landscape. Additionally, influencers often have a deep understanding of current trends and can help brands stay relevant and connected to their audience.

However, it's essential for brands to choose the right influencer for their campaigns. Factors such as authenticity, audience engagement, and relevance to the brand's values should be considered when selecting an influencer partner. Additionally, influencer marketing should be approached with transparency and ethical practices, as the credibility of both the influencer and the brand is at stake.

In conclusion, influencers play a vital role in social media advertising by effectively reaching target audiences, bringing authenticity to campaigns, and providing unique content. Working with influencers can help companies increase brand awareness, engagement, and ultimately drive sales.

Identifying Relevant Influencers for Brand Partnerships

When it comes to identifying relevant influencers for brand partnerships, there are a few steps you can follow to ensure success:

Define your target audience: Start by clearly identifying who your target audience is. This will help you understand the type of influencers that will best resonate with your brand's message and reach the right audience.

Research and analyze: Conduct thorough research to find influencers who align with your brand values, have a strong online presence, and engage with their followers. Look at their content, audience demographics, engagement rates, and previous brand collaborations to assess their suitability.

Use influencer platforms: Utilize influencer platforms like NinjaOutreach, Upfluence, or BuzzSumo to discover influencers in your niche. These platforms often provide detailed analytics and insights to help you make informed decisions.

Vet their authenticity: It's important to evaluate an influencer's authenticity and credibility. Check for fake followers or engagement by analyzing the quality of their audience interactions, comment sections, and response rates.

Reach out with a personalized pitch: Once you've shortlisted potential influencers, craft a personalized pitch that highlights the mutual benefit of a brand partnership. Clearly outline your brand values, objectives, and expectations, demonstrating how the collaboration can be a win-win for both parties.

Build relationships: Successful influencer partnerships are built on strong relationships. Take the time to engage with influencers through comments, shares, and direct messages. This will help establish a rapport and show genuine interest in their work.

Track and measure results: After partnering with influencers, track and measure the success of your campaigns. Check key performance indicators like engagement rates, website traffic, and conversions to assess the effectiveness of the partnership.

Remember, finding the perfect influencer takes time and effort. It's crucial to choose influencers who align with your brand's values, have an engaged audience, and can help amplify your message to achieve the desired impact.

Negotiating Collaborations and Managing Influencer Campaigns

Negotiating collaborations and managing influencer campaigns can be an effective strategy for growing your brand's visibility and reaching target audiences.

Here are some steps to help navigate this process:

Define your goals: Clearly outline what you hope to achieve through the collaboration or influencer campaign. Whether it's increased brand awareness, generating sales, or reaching new demographics, understanding your objectives will guide your approach.

Identify potential collaborators or influencers: Research individuals or brands that align with your values and target audience. Look at their engagement rates, follower demographics, and content quality to ensure a good fit. Compile a list of potential partners to approach.

Craft a compelling pitch: When reaching out to potential collaborators or influencers, emphasize how the collaboration is mutually beneficial. Highlight what sets your brand apart and how it aligns with their audience. Personalize your pitch to make it stand out and showcase why they should collaborate with you.

Negotiate terms: Once you've identified interested parties, negotiate the terms of the collaboration or influencer campaign. This includes discussing deliverables, compensation, timelines, exclusivity, and any contractual obligations. Be open to compromise and find a mutually beneficial agreement.

Execute the campaign: Once the terms are settled, provide the necessary resources, such as product samples or creative assets, and set clear expectations for both parties. Regularly communicate and offer support throughout the campaign to ensure its success.

Evaluate and adjust: After the campaign has concluded, evaluate its performance based on your predetermined goals. Look at key metrics like engagement rates, website traffic, and conversions. Collect feedback from the collaborators or influencers to make improvements for future campaigns.

Remember, building meaningful collaborations and executing influencer campaigns is an ongoing process. Continuously assess your strategies, adapt to market trends, and forge new partnerships to maximize results.

Influencer marketing has grown significantly in recent years but measuring its impact and return on investment (ROI) can be challenging. However, by following a systematic approach and utilizing various metrics, you can gauge the effectiveness of your influencer marketing efforts.

Here are some steps to consider:

Set clear goals: Define what you want to achieve through influencer marketing, such as increasing brand awareness, driving website traffic, or boosting sales. Having specific goals will help you measure the impact accurately.

Track engagement metrics: Monitor key engagement metrics like likes, comments, shares, and click-through rates to assess how well your influencer content is resonating with your target audience. Social media analytics tools can provide insights into these metrics.

Analyze website traffic: Use tools like Google Analytics to track the number of visitors, time spent on site, bounce rate, and conversion rates resulting from influencer-driven traffic. This will give you insights into the effectiveness of your influencer marketing campaigns in driving website engagement.

Measure sales and revenue: Implement custom tracking links or unique discount codes to track the number of conversions and sales directly attributed to influencer marketing. By monitoring the generated revenue and comparing it with your investment in influencers, you can calculate the ROI of your campaigns.

Conduct surveys and feedback: Obtain feedback from your target audience through surveys or interviews to understand their perceptions of your brand and how influencer marketing has influenced their decision-making process. This qualitative data can complement the quantitative metrics and provide valuable insights.

Compare performance across influencers: Monitor the performance of different influencers on various campaigns or content collaborations. Assess their reach, engagement levels, and the impact they have on your brand. This will help you identify which influencers are generating the most significant results for your investment.

Use an influencer management platform: Utilize influencer management platforms that can aggregate data, provide analytics, and assist in tracking and measuring the effectiveness of your campaigns. These platforms can streamline the process and provide valuable insights for ROI calculation.

Remember, influencer marketing is not solely about immediate sales but also about building brand reputation, increasing loyalty, and establishing long-term relationships with your target audience. By combining quantitative and qualitative analysis, you can better understand the impact and ROI of your influencer marketing efforts.

CHAPTER 9: STAYING AHEAD OF SOCIAL MEDIA ADVERTISING TRENDS

Emerging Trends in Social Media Advertising and Digital Marketing

In the ever-evolving world of social media advertising and digital marketing, there are several emerging trends that businesses and marketers should keep an eye on.

Here are a few of them:

Influencer Marketing: Collaborating with social media influencers who have a dedicated following has become a popular strategy for brands. This trend is expected to continue as influencers can help businesses reach their target audience in a more authentic and engaging way.

Personalization and User-generated Content: With the rise of big data and AI, personalizing marketing messages has become more feasible. Tailoring ads based on user preferences and behavior can greatly enhance the effectiveness of campaigns. Additionally, user-generated content, such as customer reviews and testimonials, can be leveraged to build trust with potential customers.

Video Content Dominance: The popularity of video content on social media platforms has skyrocketed. Short-form videos, live streaming, and interactive content are being favored by users and can be utilized by marketers to grab attention and convey their brand message effectively.

Augmented Reality (AR): AR technology is becoming more accessible, allowing businesses to integrate it into their marketing efforts. Augmented reality filters and experiences can enhance brand engagement and create memorable interactions with consumers.

Social Commerce: Social media platforms are increasingly incorporating e-commerce features such as in-app purchases and shoppable posts. This enables businesses to streamline the customer journey from discovery to purchase, making social commerce a significant trend to watch.

Voice Search Optimization: The growing popularity of voice assistants like Siri, Alexa, and Google Home has made voice search optimization crucial for businesses. Optimizing content for voice search queries can help brands capture more visibility and remain relevant in an increasingly voice-first world.

These are just a few of the emerging trends transforming social media advertising and digital marketing. It's essential for businesses to stay informed, adapt, and experiment with these trends to stay competitive in the ever-changing landscape.

Utilizing New Ad Formats and Features Offered by Platforms

When it comes to maximizing your advertising efforts, staying up to date with the latest ad formats and features offered by platforms is crucial. These advancements can provide unique opportunities to enhance your campaigns and engage with your target audience in more effective ways.

Here are a few key points to consider:

Research and stay informed: Keep yourself informed about the latest advertising options available on different platforms. This could include features like interactive ads, augmented reality experiences, or even new ad placements. Regularly visit the platforms' official blogs or attend industry events to gather insights and stay ahead of the curve.

Understand your audience: Before diving into new ad formats, it's essential to have a deep understanding of your target audience. Consider their demographics, preferences, and behaviors. This knowledge will help you choose the most suitable ad formats and features to effectively capture their attention and drive engagement.

Test and experiment: Once you have identified some promising ad formats and features, it's crucial to test and experiment with them. Start with smaller budgets and measure the performance of these ads against your key performance indicators (KPIs). This will allow you to understand their impact and make data-driven decisions about scaling your efforts.

Leverage automation and data analysis: As an assistant, I highly recommend utilizing automation tools and platforms that offer robust data analysis capabilities. These tools can help you optimize your campaigns, target specific audience segments, and track important metrics. Additionally, they can provide valuable insights into the effectiveness of different ad formats, allowing you to make informed adjustments and improvements.

Stay creative and adapt: While it's essential to embrace new ad formats and features, don't forget the power of creativity. Experiment with different creative elements, messaging, and visuals to captivate your audience. Regularly analyze the results and make necessary adjustments to deliver compelling campaigns.

Remember, successful advertising requires continuous learning, adaptation, and staying on top of industry trends. By exploring new ad formats and features, you can enhance your campaigns and achieve better results in reaching and engaging with your target audience.

Incorporating Video, Live Streaming, and Interactive Ad Content

Video content, live streaming, and interactive ad content are powerful tools for engaging and captivating audiences in today's digital landscape. By incorporating these elements into your marketing strategies, you can effectively communicate your message, attract attention, and drive conversions.

Here's how each of these components can contribute to your overall success:

Video Content: Videos have become increasingly popular due to their ability to convey information in an engaging and visually appealing manner. Whether you're creating product demos, how-to guides, or brand stories, videos can effectively capture your audience's attention and deliver your message effectively. Keep your videos concise, visually appealing, and optimized for different platforms, ensuring they are accessible across various devices.

Live Streaming: Live streaming allows you to connect with your audience in real-time, fostering a sense of authenticity and interactivity. Whether you're hosting live events, Q&A sessions, interviews, or behind-the-scenes glimpses, live streaming helps create a unique and immersive experience. Promote your live streams in advance, encourage audience participation through comments and questions, and ensure a reliable internet connection for a seamless experience.

Interactive Ad Content: Interactive ad content encourages active participation from viewers, making them more likely to remember and engage with your brand. Interactive ads can include gamification elements, surveys, quizzes, or augmented reality experiences. By providing an interactive and personalized experience, you can enhance brand awareness, gather valuable data, and increase overall customer engagement.

When using these elements, it's essential to consider your target audience, platforms, and the goals you want to achieve. Make sure your content aligns with your brand identity, remains authentic, and provides value to your viewers. Regularly analyze and optimize your strategies based on audience feedback and data insights to continually improve your results.

Remember, the key is to create compelling, well-structured, and cohesive content that resonates with your audience, encourages active participation, and ultimately drives your desired outcomes.

Leveraging Artificial Intelligence and Automation for Efficient Campaigns

In today's digital era, harnessing the power of artificial intelligence (AI) and automation can greatly enhance the efficiency of your campaigns. By leveraging these technologies, you can streamline processes, optimize targeting, and increase overall effectiveness.

Here's how:

Data-driven insights: AI can analyze vast amounts of data to identify patterns, trends, and audience preferences. By leveraging this information, you can make data-driven decisions and create highly targeted campaigns that resonate with your audience.

Personalization at scale: Automation tools enable you to create personalized content and experiences for each individual in your target audience, at scale. This level of customization can significantly enhance engagement and conversion rates.

Automated campaign management: AI-powered tools can handle repetitive tasks such as ad placement, budget allocation, and performance monitoring. This frees up your time and resources while ensuring optimal campaign management.

Predictive analytics: AI algorithms can predict future consumer behavior based on historical data. By leveraging these insights, you can optimize your campaign strategies and allocate resources to the most promising avenues.

Chatbot assistance: Chatbots, powered by AI, can assist customers throughout their journey, from answering queries to providing personalized recommendations. This improves customer satisfaction and increases the chances of conversion.

A/B testing and optimization: AI tools can automate the process of A/B testing, allowing you to quickly identify the most effective messaging, design, or targeting approach. This enables continuous optimization and improved campaign performance.

Language translation and localization: AI-powered translation tools can help you translate your campaigns into multiple languages quickly and accurately, allowing you to effectively target global audiences.

By leveraging AI and automation, you can not only save time and resources but also create more impactful, targeted campaigns. With the ability to analyze data, personalize content, and automate processes, these technologies pave the way for efficient and successful campaigns in today's competitive landscape.

Conclusion:

To ensure effective social media marketing, it's important to follow key strategies and best practices.

Here is a recap:

Define your goals: Clearly outline what you want to achieve through your social media advertising campaigns. Whether it's increasing brand awareness, driving website traffic, or generating leads, having a clear goal will help you tailor your strategy.

Know your target audience: Understanding your audience's demographics, interests, and behaviors will enable you to create more relevant and engaging ads. Utilize social media analytics and audience insights to gather this information.

Choose the right platforms: Different social media platforms cater to different demographics and interests. Identify which platforms your target audience uses the most and invest in those platforms to maximize your reach.

Develop engaging creatives: Catch the attention of your audience with compelling visuals, videos, and copy. Use eye-catching graphics and concise, persuasive language to communicate your message effectively.

A/B testing: Experiment with different ad variations to identify what resonates best with your audience. Test different visuals, headlines, ad formats, and calls-to-action to optimize your advertising performance.

Use targeting options: Leverage social media advertising platforms' targeting options to reach the right audience. Narrow down your target audience based on location, demographics, interests, and even behavior.

Utilize remarketing: Implement remarketing ads to reach users who have shown interest in your brand or website. This strategy can help drive conversions by reinforcing your message to users who have already engaged with your content.

Monitor and optimize performance: Regularly review your campaign metrics and make data-driven decisions. Adjust your targeting, creative elements, and budget based on what performs best to improve your campaign's effectiveness.

Set a budget and schedule: Define a budget that aligns with your goals and allocate it effectively across different campaigns. Additionally, consider scheduling your ads during peak engagement times to maximize their visibility.

Stay up to date with trends: Social media advertising is constantly evolving. Stay current with industry trends, algorithm updates, and new ad formats to stay ahead of the competition and make the most of your campaigns.

By following these strategies and best practices, you can enhance the effectiveness of your social media advertising campaigns and achieve your desired results.

Continuous Testing, Learning, and Adapting

Continuous testing, learning, and adapting to changing trends are crucial for personal growth, professional development, and overall success in today's dynamic world.

Here's why these practices are so important:

Staying Relevant: In a fast-paced and ever-evolving world, trends and technologies are constantly changing. By continuously testing, learning, and adapting, individuals and businesses can stay up to date with the latest developments, ensuring they remain relevant in their respective fields. This allows them to stay competitive and seize new opportunities.

Identifying Gaps and Improving Skills: Continuous testing helps identify gaps in knowledge or skills. Regularly evaluating one's performance, seeking feedback, and analyzing results enable individuals to recognize areas that need improvement.

By actively learning and acquiring new skills, they can bridge these gaps, enhance their abilities, and grow both personally and professionally.

Embracing Innovation: Adapting to changing trends involves an openness to new ideas and innovation. By being willing to explore emerging technologies, methodologies, and approaches, individuals can facilitate progress, discover innovative solutions, and gain a competitive edge. This mindset encourages creativity and fosters a culture of innovation within organizations.

Anticipating and Responding to Change: Adapting to changing trends allows individuals and businesses to anticipate and respond effectively to shifts in the market. By staying ahead of the curve, they can proactively address challenges, identify opportunities, and make informed decisions. This agility helps them navigate unpredictable situations, mitigate risks, and maintain long-term sustainability.

Continuous Improvement: Testing, learning, and adapting promote a culture of continuous improvement. By regularly evaluating processes, products, and strategies, individuals and organizations can identify inefficiencies, refine approaches, and optimize performance. This iterative process ensures that they constantly strive for excellence, driving growth and success over time.

Final Thoughts

In conclusion, the art of strategic social media marketing has become an essential tool for businesses in today's digital landscape. By leveraging the immense reach and targeting capabilities of platforms like Facebook, Instagram, and Twitter, businesses can effectively engage with their target audience, drive brand awareness, and ultimately increase conversions and sales. However, it is crucial to approach social media advertising with a well-defined strategy in order to maximize its potential.

This includes setting clear objectives, understanding the

target audience, creating compelling and relevant content, and continuously monitoring and optimizing campaigns based on data-driven insights. With the right approach, businesses can unlock the true power of social media advertising and achieve remarkable results.

So, embrace the art of strategic social media marketing and take your brand to new heights in the digital age!

ABOUT THE AUTHOR

Kimberly Hodge

As a retired career college instructor in the wellness field, Kimberly has a vast amount of knowledge in health and wellness topics. In addition, she also has many years of experience owning and operating several successful small businesses. She now focuses on her writing. She enjoys writing in the health and wellness, business, and spiritual genre. When Kimberly is not writing she enjoys spending time with her husband and their fur baby.

BOOKS BY THIS AUTHOR

Art Of The Strategic Passive Income Stream: 50 Ideas Of Making Passive Income

Are you tired of the daily grind and longing for a way to escape the 9 to 5 rat race? Look no further! Discover the power of passive income and take control of your financial future.

Passive income is not just a pipe dream; it's a tangible reality that anyone can achieve. Imagine earning money while you sleep, travel, or spend time with loved ones. It's time to turn your aspirations into actions and embark on a journey towards financial freedom. But where do you start? The first step is to educate yourself.

So, are you ready to break free from the chains of traditional income and create a life of financial freedom? Are you ready to take control of your destiny and build a legacy that will benefit not only yourself but also future generations?

Imagine waking up every morning knowing that you have multiple streams of income working for you, even while you sleep. Picture the peace of mind that comes with having financial stability and the ability to pursue your passions without worrying about money.

The Art Of Strategic Leadership And Management

In this book, the keyword "leadership and management" takes

center stage as a beacon of guidance in today's ever-changing world. As we delve into its pages, we unearth the profound significance of these concepts in shaping organizations towards triumph.

With every turn of its pages, our minds are invigorated by key principles that ignite passion within us; they serve as steppingstones towards becoming visionary leaders who inspire greatness among their teams.

The author skillfully unravels the intricacies of leadership and management, unraveling secrets to unlocking hidden potential within individuals and forging them into formidable units bound for success.

This thrilling journey offers invaluable tips that act like secret weapons enabling us to adapt swiftly to challenges, foster collaboration amidst diversity, and nurture innovation with contagious enthusiasm.

This book becomes an exhilarating catalyst propelling readers towards achieving extraordinary accomplishments rooted in effective leadership techniques – making it an essential compass for those seeking transformative successes!

The Art Of Strategic Goal Setting And Time Management

Unlocking the secrets to effective time management and strategic goal setting is like discovering a hidden treasure chest filled with endless possibilities. In today's fast-paced world, where every second counts, mastering the art of balancing priorities and maximizing productivity has become essential for success in both personal and professional spheres.

Whether you're an entrepreneur striving to achieve your business goals, or a student aiming to excel academically, understanding how to set strategic goals and manage your time can be the key that unlocks a world of opportunities.

In this book post, we will dive deep into the importance of goal setting as a powerful time management tool. We'll explore the theory and psychology behind goal setting, uncovering why planning is vital and how it impacts problem-solving abilities.

Art Of The Strategic Side Hustle: Simple Steps To Developing A Passive Income Side Hustle

Passive income, oh what a glorious concept it is! It holds the key to unlocking the doors of financial freedom and establishing a life filled with abundance. Picture this: in a world where money tirelessly flows into your bank account without you lifting a finger, opportunities become limitless, and dreams turn into tangible realities. The significance of passive income lies within its ability to liberate us from the shackles of traditional employment.

No longer bound by trading time for money, we are free to pursue our passions, explore new ventures, and spend quality time with loved ones. This mystical force allows us to break away from the monotonous cycle of living paycheck to paycheck; it grants us the power to take control of our own destinies and create lasting wealth that will sustain generations to come.

Passive income serves as both mentor and guide on our journey towards financial independence - encouraging us to think beyond conventional norms, inspiring innovation, and fostering an unwavering belief in ourselves. So, let's embrace this exhilarating dance with destiny as we embark on a path paved with passive income riches!

The Strategic Home-Based Business Guide: A Practical Guide To Starting A Home-Based Business

Have you ever dreamed of taking control of your own destiny and breaking free from the constraints of a traditional office job? Well, brace yourself for the exciting possibilities that lie ahead! Starting a home-based business is like embarking on an exhilarating adventure filled with endless opportunities. Imagine waking up each morning to the sweet aroma of freshly brewed coffee as you step into your cozy home office, ready to conquer the world in your pajamas.

With this book at your fingertips, you have the power to turn your passions and talents into a thriving enterprise right from the comfort of your own abode. No more commuting through congested traffic or dealing with never-ending cubicle walls stifling creativity; instead, you can design a workspace tailored to inspire and motivate you towards achieving greatness.

Whether it's providing innovative services, crafting unique products, or becoming an influential content creator, starting a home-based business opens doors to boundless potential while granting you unparalleled flexibility and freedom. So why settle for ordinary when extraordinary awaits? Take that leap today and unlock a future brimming with excitement!

The Strategic Work From Home Guide

The exciting possibilities of remotely working from home offer a tantalizing glimpse into a future where freedom and productivity coexist harmoniously. Imagine waking up to the gentle kiss of sunlight streaming through your bedroom window, knowing that your office is just a few steps away from the next room.

With remote work, you can bid farewell to soul-crushing commutes and embrace the blissful flexibility of managing your own schedule. Whether it's taking breaks to walk barefoot on the soft grass outside or enjoying impromptu dance parties in between tasks, the perks are endless!

The benefits extend beyond mere convenience; they encompass increased job satisfaction and improved mental well-being. By eliminating distractions common in traditional office environments, telecommuting empowers individuals to fully immerse themselves in their work while finding a healthy balance with personal life demands.

Welcome aboard this exhilarating journey into a world brimming with limitless opportunities!

www.ingramcontent.com/pod-product-compliance
Lightning Source LLC
Chambersburg PA
CBHW072341290526
45794CB00002B/961